FIRST DYNASTY MINDSET

Published by BooxAi

ISBN: 978-965-578-419-0

FIRST DYNASTY MINDSET

UNLEASHING THE LIGHT WITHIN THE POWER
OF THOUGHT

GEORGE A. DENNIS JR.

CONTENTS

AUTHOR BIO: GEORGE DENNIS JR.

George Dennis Jr. is a visionary author, a father, and a spiritual being having a human experience and is on a mission to bring positive transformation to his community and beyond. Born into a lineage of wisdom and ancient knowledge, his ancestry can be traced back to the legendary figure of George William Gordon, an esteemed advocate for wealth, justice, and empowerment during his time, and one the wealthiest men in the Caribbean. Raised in the vibrant city of Minneapolis, Minnesota, he grew up surrounded by stories of his family's rich history and of their profound impact on the lives of those around them. These narratives, coupled with his own personal experiences and spiritual journey, ignited a deep passion within him to carry on the legacy of his ancestors.

Driven by a thirst for knowledge and a desire to uplift his community. Drawing inspiration from these profound insights, George began to shape a new narrative that would empower individuals to embrace their innate power and create positive change in their lives.

As a Performance coach, mentor, and Business coach, he uses his wisdom and expertise to inspire others to tap into their true potential and embrace a life of abundance, fulfillment, and purpose. He believes that by harnessing the power of their thoughts and aligning with universal principles, individuals can transcend limitations and co-create their reality.

Through his engaging and insightful writing, the author seeks to share these transformative teachings with his community, guiding them toward a brighter future and a deeper connection to their authentic selves. His work embodies the essence of the First Dynasty Mindset, a philosophy that fosters self-belief, holistic growth, and the pursuit of abundant living.

PROLOGUE: UNLEASHING THE LIGHT WITHIN

Welcome to the enchanting world of the First Dynasty Mindset. Today, we embark on an extraordinary journey—a journey that transcends the boundaries of ordinary existence and is immersed in the infinite realm of our thoughts, beliefs, and their profound impact. As the curtain rises on our journey, we are introduced to the timeless wisdom of First Dynasty philosophy—a treasure trove of principles that lay the foundation for our transformation. In the essence of these profound teachings, we uncover the Law of Mentalism, which reverberates with the notion that our thoughts are the architects of our physical, spiritual, and financial reality. Within this universal truth lies the key to attaining the riches we desire, and overcoming the challenges like illnesses, addiction, and diseases that may beset our path.

As we delve deeper into the heart of the First Dynasty Mindset, we are captivated by the spellbinding revelations that unfold before us. We bear witness to the astonishing power of positive thinking, intention setting, and the art of visualization—potent tools that enable us to magnetize wealth, health, and prosperity into our lives. In the realm of our thoughts, we discover an unparalleled reservoir of creative potential, capable of shaping the course of our financial journey.

Yet, amidst the wisdom lies the enigma—the self-limiting beliefs that cloud our vision and hinder our financial and personal growth. The First Dynasty Mindset beckons us to confront these formidable barriers head-on, for it is in this transformative confrontation that we unearth the true essence of our being. Armed with the principles of First Dynasty philosophy, we learn to transform these limiting beliefs into empowering ones, propelling us toward the zenith of financial, physical, and spiritual success.

Throughout our expedition, we will encounter an individual whose stories resonate with the symphony of human resilience and triumph. We are humbled by the fortitude of those who, against all odds, harnessed the power of their thoughts and beliefs to rise above all challenges and embrace abundance. His stories are a testament to the boundless potential within each of us—a potential waiting to be unleashed.

And so, I extend a heartfelt invitation to each of you, dear companions, in this captivating odyssey—a journey where the human spirit soars to great heights and touches the firmament of financial, physical, and spiritual success. With unwavering belief, we shall traverse the landscape of our thoughts, guided by the principles of the FIRST DYNASTY philosophy. As we embark upon this transformative quest, we must remember that it is not only for personal gain but to inspire, uplift, and transform the lives of those around us. Today marks the genesis of an extraordinary voyage—one that transcends the boundaries of ordinary existence. Together, we shall unravel the mysteries that lie within our minds and unearth the immeasurable wealth that resides within us.

1

THE LEGACY UNVEILED - UNLEASHING THE POWER WITHIN

In the bustling diverse city of Minneapolis, Minnesota, a young man named George found himself at a crossroads in life. Despite being unaware that he was a descendant of an ancient lineage known as "The First Dynasty," a family that held secrets to unlocking the power of wealth and abundance through the mind. George felt trapped in a cycle of self-doubt and limited opportunities. At the time, the city was in a civil rights movement, and a police-involved death of an unarmed man with the same name died in the same neighborhood as he grew up. He was looking for a way out of these environments of lack, death, despair, and confusion. An official girl dad, with three 3 kids, 1 boy, and 2 girls. In George's mind, he knew it was his time to shine. Little did he know that his journey to discovering "The Light Within" and mastering his inner dialogue would transform his life and the lives of future generations.

He had always been aware of his family's rich heritage and the knowledge they possessed. Stories of their incredible wealth and prosperity had been passed down through generations, and he grew up hearing these tales with awe and intrigue. However, as he stood at the threshold of parenthood, he could not help but feel a deep sense of disconnection from the abundance that was his birthright.

George would ask his father about the stories and if they were true. His father always replied with the same answer, yes but we don't have proof anymore. It was a family vacation to Jamaica where he went to his grandfather's house. A beautiful house built by his grandfather and his uncles. The ancestral home sat dominantly on a hill called Marley Mount.

His grandfather had recently passed and left him a box in the attic. It was a tough time for the family, with over 100 family members present. Thinking only of the loss of his loved ones, George doubted his family would ever be rich again. All the family did was argue and bicker a lot, quarreling over scraps. "How did we fall from grace?" he thought to himself. When a serendipitous moment happened. He decided to go up to the dark dusty attic. upon discovery of the box, there was a hidden book, a treasure—an ancient family archive tucked away in the box in the attic of his ancestral home. As he dusted off the cobwebs and opened the worn leather cover, he discovered it was dated 1857. Signed by George W. Gordon, a book of ancient wisdom, wealth, and secret teachings that were passed down over 6 thousand years through the generations. The chills and anxiety George received by holding such a relic. These teachings emphasized the power of thought, the principles of the First Dynasty mindset ideology, and the limitless potential that resided within everyone.

At that moment, George knew he had uncovered a priceless treasure—an opportunity to transcend his current circumstances and step into a life of unlimited abundance. Until then, he realized the stories of his great-great-grandfather being the wealthiest man in the Caribbean were true. The last known family member to possess this book Was George William Gordon. George William Gordon his great-great-grandfather was revered as his Excellency, a legend, icon, businesses man, business owner, and landowner. It was then He dedicated himself to being a student and mastering the teachings of "The First Dynasty" and embracing the mindset that had been entrusted to him.

Through his exploration of the archive, George began to understand the profound connection between his thoughts and his physical reality. He learned that his beliefs, attitudes, and perceptions shaped the world he experienced. With this newfound awareness, he realized that words or thoughts like "I'm tired of being broke," were a thought, not to think ever! He knew he held the key to transforming his life and manifesting the wealth he desired. He believed that if he could control even the tiniest of thoughts and even wield those little thoughts, he would see dreams come true.

As he immersed himself in the wisdom of "The First Dynasty," and discovered the powers of intention and visualization. One of the secrets was the Body could not tell the difference between an imagined thought and a dream or reality. Meaning he could trick his body into believing in the state desired before it manifested. In other words, he discovered this technique gave the body the future experience ahead of reality now rather than later. Why would George do this? Envisioning it and having replicated the exact feeling of that dream, desire, idea, or vision, made the body more magnetic in the universal fields of opportunities. It was the breakthrough he needed. The key finally. He learned to clarify his goals and set clear intentions for what he wanted to manifest in his life. By consistently focusing his thoughts and directing his energy towards his desired outcomes, he witnessed the remarkable power of thought in shaping his reality.

George's journey was not without its challenges. He encountered moments of doubt and faced setbacks along the way. It was 2021, and the location was Minneapolis Minnesota. The environment was less than favorable. Shootings, riots, more police brutality, and senseless violence took siege of the twin cities. Yet, armed with the teachings of "The First Dynasty" and the unwavering belief in his potential, he persevered. He understood that every challenge was an opportunity for growth, and every setback was a stepping stone toward his ultimate success.

Through his experiences, he discovered that true wealth extended beyond mere monetary possessions. It encompassed a sense of purpose, fulfillment, and a deep connection to one's inner self. He learned to cultivate gratitude for the abundance that already existed in his life and to share his wealth with others, knowing that the act of giving only multiplied his blessings.

As George continued to align himself with the principles of "The First Dynasty," he witnessed a profound transformation in his reality once more. Opportunities began to unfold before him, synchronicities became a regular occurrence, and abundance flowed into his life effortlessly. His mother became worried and asked, "How is this possible?"

The teachings of "The First Dynasty" are timeless and universal, applicable to anyone who seeks to unlock their full potential and experience the abundance they deserve. The power of thought knows no bounds, and the principles of First Dynasty philosophy transcend time and space.

How did he do it? He finally told his mom about the book she had accidentally thrown out. It goes back to 1865 when the last entry was frequency.

This was George's secret, how he was moving faster, getting more opportunities like his great-great-grandfather. He spent more time on the thoughts of the future than memories of the past. Emotions, doubt, dreams, hate, abundance, and all things resonated on a frequency. He acted, pretending to already have his desires met, and feeling wholeness.

2

—————

THE POWER OF THOUGHT AND INTENTION - MANIFESTING ABUNDANCE

As the author delved deeper into the teachings of his ancestral archive, he learned that his thoughts functioned as seeds planted in the fertile soil of the universal mind, ready to germinate and bear fruit in the form of reality. The danger of this knowledge did not care if you were aware of it or not. It grows It could be negative ideas, poison ivy, nightshade, hate, fear, doubt, and excuses, it grows. He knew Guided by the principles of the First Dynasty mindset, he understood the significance of aligning his thoughts with abundance, becoming familiar with wholeness, peacefulness, pretending, and practicing the emotions and feelings of having money, land, luxury cars, and good health all that aligned with his deepest desires were all frequencies.

In the realm of the First Dynasty Mindset, the pursuit of material abundance is not merely a quest for possessions, but a dynamic interplay between the external and the internal, a reflection of the power of thoughts, beliefs, and actions. It is a journey that George, the torchbearer of ancient wisdom, embarks upon, weaving together the fabric of tangible wealth and intangible mastery.

As he delves into the realms of prosperity consciousness, he recognizes that material abundance is a manifestation of his inner world. The luxurious penthouses, gleaming vehicles, and exquisite artifacts are not merely status symbols; they are reflections of his alignment with the principles of the universe. In this pursuit, he understands that his thoughts are the architects, his beliefs are the blueprints, and his actions are the construction crew.

One cornerstone of George's material accumulation is his unwavering belief in the abundance that surrounds him. Through the First Dynasty Mindset, he comprehends that scarcity is an illusion, a result of limited thinking. As he shifts his thoughts towards the limitless, he witnesses how his reality mirrors his mindset. The more he visualizes himself in possession of his desired material wealth, the more he attracts circumstances that facilitate their realization.

Armed with this newfound knowledge, George became aware of the quality of his thoughts. He realized that each thought he entertained influenced the energy he emitted into the world. He knew it was already scientific proof of the body being able to generate a first-world country for at least one year. He saw how negative thoughts bred doubt and scarcity, while positive thoughts nurtured confidence and abundance.

To cultivate a Dynasty mindset, George began to plant seeds of abundance in the garden of his mind. He replaced self-limiting beliefs with empowering affirmations that reminded him of his worthiness for success and prosperity. He nurtured thoughts of abundance, becoming familiar with self-love, and self-improvement, observing the thoughts he called seeds, George would water them and give them proper sun. And whenever weeds would show up, we called bad or negative thoughts, they were immediately rooted out. Bad thoughts or negative thinking are seeds as well, blowing in the wind. He was mindful of what was blowing in the wind, so he was very protective of his mind. He did not allow people's thoughts to be good or bad to influence him unless it was aligned with his beliefs. With this technique of gardening the mind, George was able to have dominion, prosper and subdue his reality and his world. He no longer abandoned his thoughts to negativity and darkness.

3

THE LAW OF ATTRACTION: A
MAGNETIC FORCE

While cultivating his First Dynasty mindset, he soon encountered the Law of Mentalism—a universal principle that responds to the energy of our thoughts and intentions. He learned that like attracts like and that his dominant thoughts functioned as a magnetic force, attracting corresponding circumstances and experiences. But the secret was the magnet, the body was the magnet. The environments signal the genes, and a gene is expressed as an emotion, feeling, or memory. If you understand the law of correspondence, you can reverse this process through thoughts and feelings imagined. What George understood is that while people used the term "seeing is believing," He reworded the phrase to "believe to seeing." He believed in the thing first, with all the emotions of having it already, then he would see it. After that seeing is easy, believing was the true test.

This was proven when George's father was diagnosed with cancer, with 8% heart function. When nothing else worked, that day George told his father to keep imagining how it feels to be free of cancer. Then George instructed his father to be grateful for the cancer being gone five minutes at night and in the morning. George asked, "What would you do and how would you act? and feel?" George said to act like that person during the day. Grateful every day for things in the future vs the past. The trick was to think greater than you were feeling. He knew in the family archive the scrolls showed studies in the field of epigenetics that have revealed that our thoughts and emotions can influence the expression of our genes. While our genetic makeup remains largely fixed, certain genes can be "turned on" or "turned off" based on environmental factors, including our thoughts and experiences. This process is known as gene expression, which comes out to be a feeling, and it can have a significant impact on our health and well-being.

The family archive has shown that chronic stress and negative thinking can lead to changes in gene expression that are associated with increased inflammation and a weakened immune system. On the other hand, positive thinking and a sense of well-being have been linked to changes in gene expression that promote better health and resilience.

Moreover, our thoughts and emotions can also influence the body's biofield, an electromagnetic field that extends beyond its physical boundaries. The biofield is generated by the activity of the body's cells and organs, and it interacts with the environment around us.

The family archive suggested that positive emotions, such as gratitude and love, create a coherent and harmonious biofield, while negative emotions disrupt their coherence. A coherent biofield is more effective in interacting with the environment which may attract opportunities that match our energetic state.

Two weeks later he found his father gardening and mowing the lawn as if he had beaten cancer. At the next appointment, George's father beat cancer with 8% heart function. George's father is more than 12 months cancer free 99% heart function, and all on the power of thought.

All the things that were imagined manifested with speed and abundance. George was increasing the frequency in the body, so when things happened, it looked organic and natural. It looked and felt as if it would have happened anyway to someone on the outside looking in. As he practiced this principle, he observed how synchronicities and opportunities seemed to effortlessly flow into his life.

4

THE POWER OF INTENTION: SETTING THE COURSE

With the Law of Mentalism as his ally, he understood the importance of setting clear intentions for wealth-building. He knew that intentions functioned as the course he charted for his journey—like a commercial pilot, he or she must do a pre-flight inspection and systems checklist before taking off, George knew in life every morning you need a mental inspection of thoughts, and systems checklist of things you planned to do when you woke up. The pilot knew every time he or she did that, they took off safely and landed at the desired destination safely. You must perform a preflight checklist before you begin your day. A routine that led him toward his desired destination. George did this mentally every morning.

By setting precise intentions, he harnessed the power of his focus. He visualized himself achieving his goals, feeling the emotions of success as if they were already his reality. With each mental morning, he gave 3-5 minutes of thankfulness and things he was grateful for in the future with the intention he set, that the longer he resided in that mental state during the day, the more he sent out a beacon of energy that beckoned the universe to conspire in his favor. The First Dynasty mindset.

5

TRANSFORMING THE INNER DIALOGUE: A SHIFT IN PERCEPTION

As George trained his mind to focus on abundance and success, he experienced a profound shift in his inner dialogue. The negative self-talk that once held him from abundance. His thoughts have now been replaced with empowering conversations. He affirmed his potential, acknowledging his ability to co-create and create wealth and prosperity.

With this inner transformation, George observed how his external circumstances mirrored his newfound beliefs. Opportunities seemed to gravitate toward him, and he made decisions with confidence and clarity. The world around him responded to his positive energy, opening doors he once thought were beyond his reach.

6

PRACTICING GRATITUDE: FERTILIZING THE SEEDS OF ABUNDANCE

In the pursuit of financial success, George also realized the significance of gratitude in his grandfather's teaching. He recognized that gratitude functioned as a powerful fertilizer, nourishing the seeds of abundance he had planted in his mind. He cultivated an attitude of thankfulness, acknowledging the blessings he already possessed.

As George expressed gratitude for even the smallest victories, he noticed a positive shift in his overall outlook on life. He found joy in the journey, celebrating progress and milestones along the way. This gratitude radiated the magnetic energy that attracted even more reasons to be thankful.

7

———————

INTEGRATING THE PRINCIPLES: A SYMPHONY OF THOUGHT AND INTENTION

Throughout his journey, George witnessed the symphony of thought and intention unfolding in his life. The principles of First Dynasty philosophy acted in harmony with the Law of Mentalism, creating a powerful force that shaped his financial, physical, and spiritual reality.

By incorporating the principles of the First Dynasty mindset into our lives and consistently practicing positive thinking, visualization, and gratitude, we can potentially influence our DNA's gene expression and the coherence of our biofield. This, in turn, can create a powerful resonance with the world around us, attracting opportunities that align with our energetic state.

The family archive showed studies of neuroplasticity and epigenetics provide intriguing evidence that our thoughts and emotions can shape not only our brain's structure but also potentially influence our DNA's gene expression.

Additionally, the coherence and expansiveness of our biofield can have an impact on the opportunities that come our way. By understanding and harnessing these scientific foundations, we have the potential to change the very fabric of our being and become magnets for opportunities, propelling ourselves toward lasting prosperity and fulfillment.

The First Dynasty Mindset taught George was not just a matter of luck or circumstance. It was a deliberate practice of aligning one's thoughts and intentions with the grand orchestra of the universe. With every thought, he composed a melody that resonated on a frequency with his deepest desires, calling forth the manifestation of his dreams and opportunities.

8

**THE INTEGRATION OF FIRST
DYNASTY PRINCIPLES**

George delved into the principles of the First Dynasty, recognizing their profound impact on wealth building. He understood the importance of mentalism, the idea that All is the mind, that the universe is mental, and that thoughts created his reality. He embraced the principle of correspondence, recognizing interconnectedness in his personal reality vs. personality had interconnectedness. All the things in his personality that he lacked reflected his personal reality and what it lacked. George changed; how he thought, how he acted, and his beliefs. Those 3 things make your personality. This was the lesson in the archive represented by a tree, a modern tree of life. It meant in the archive that the seeds or thoughts must grow downward before they grow upward. In the mind, seeds and thoughts travel down as far as possible, in this case, the body. He became a different person. He looked different, spoke differently, His beliefs were different.

A political refugee, has parents fleeing from Jamaica in hopes of opportunities, George was raised in south Minneapolis. The 1980s were turbulent times. George had all the excuses, racism, educational background, and stereotypes of having to work three times as hard for the same things as his counterparts. No more! He said. Laughing and rejoicing outside at his thoughts inside. I have already won. He thought to himself. Through the principle of polarity, he understood that challenges, setbacks, and opportunities were the fruit of the same tree. Setbacks were to seeds that bear fruit, and that the seed is made for growth, personal and spiritual growth. By embracing setbacks, he could create greater success. George knew in his family archive the book described each setback carried the seed of equal or greater opportunity.

He explored the principle of vibration, learning to raise his energetic frequency to align with the vibration of wealth and abundance of opportunities. How was this possible? George explained in the family archive, like a dream, when you are running, and you wake up sweating as if you were really running. The body does not know the difference between the dream and the imagined thought. George explained to his mother he overwhelmed his thoughts imagined, with visions of the future rather than the memories of the past. He knew that this could apply to athletes from all kinds of levels of society.

9

MASTERING THE INNER DIALOGUE,

The author transforms, as he discovers the profound impact of his self-talk and learns to harness its immense power. George also incorporated visualization techniques into his daily practice. He would vividly imagine himself achieving his goals, whenever he was picturing a place, he pictured the air in his thoughts to be pristine. He visualized abundance in the form of having so much that he would give most of it away. He would visualize the steps he needed to take and the outcomes he desired. This practice not only reinforced his positive self-talk but also ignited a sense of excitement and anticipation within him.

The biofield, also known as the body's electromagnetic field, is a real and measurable energy field that extends beyond its physical boundaries. Studies have shown that the human body emits electromagnetic waves, and these waves can interact with the environment, influencing the world around us.

As his knowledge grew and his strategies evolved, he saw his wealth steadily increase. The Luxury cars, clothes, and expensive items were of great taste. He bought fifty acres of fertile land for the family, grew businesses, and bought yachts. But more importantly, George experienced a newfound sense of Freedom and financial security, and wholeness. He knew that he had laid the groundwork for lasting wealth and that his journey was just beginning.

10

ALIGNING WITH ABUNDANCE - CULTIVATING HOLISTIC WEALTH AND EMPOWERING CONNECTIONS

As the writer delved deeper into his pursuit of financial success, he realized that wealth was not solely confined to monetary riches. No one preaches that, once you get there, the less you know. True abundance encompassed all aspects of his life: physical, emotional, and spiritual. George aligned his thoughts with abundance by nurturing his holistic well-being and forging empowering connections.

He recognized that his physical well-being played a crucial role in his overall sense of abundance. He understood that taking care of his body was an investment in his long-term success. He prioritized regular exercise, nourishing his body with healthy foods, and getting sufficient rest. By honoring his physical health, George fueled his energy levels, enhanced his focus, and created a solid foundation for sustainable growth.

But holistic wealth extended beyond the physical realm. George realized the importance of nurturing his emotional and spiritual well-being as well. He began practicing gratitude for 3 minutes in the morning, 3 minutes acknowledging, 3 more minutes appreciating the blessings, and 3 minutes being thankful for the abundance already present in his life. George shifted his focus from what he lacked to what he possessed, creating a positive mindset that attracted even more blessings day by day. This was a game-changer.

When the brain learns anything new it makes a new synaptic connection. That connection improves the brain's performance. He understood making physical connections with other minds mentally improves his performance in his physical performance. Furthermore, George recognized the transformative power of positive relationships and connections. He understood that his journey to success was not meant to travel alone. He sought out like-minded individuals who shared his vision and values, forming a supportive network of individuals on a similar path. George knew visualization played major roles in top professional athletes, actors, entertainers, politicians, community leaders, speakers, authors, doctors, students, and many more.

He nurtures positive relationships and fosters empowering connections that support everyone's journey. Together, they celebrated each other's wins, offered guidance during challenges, and created a collective energy that propelled them all toward their goals.

Now was the founding of the First Dynasty Foundation. George also understood the value of collaboration and sought opportunities to connect and collaborate with others in his industry. By aligning himself with individuals who had complementary skills and expertise, he created synergistic relationships that opened doors to new possibilities and accelerated his growth. Through collaboration, he tapped into a pearl of collective wisdom that enriched his own knowledge and expanded his horizons again. In his journey to align with abundance, George recognized the power of giving back to others.

So, he created the First Dynasty Foundation. He understood that generosity and service were to serve and to be of service to others. This ideology created a ripple effect of positive energy in his own life. George sought opportunities to contribute to causes and organizations aligned with his values, knowing that the act of giving would enrich his sense of purpose and deepen his connection with abundance.

While cultivating his holistic wealth and nurtured empowering connections, he witnessed the profound impact it had on his journey. He realized that success was not a solitary pursuit but a collective endeavor, influenced by the relationships we foster and the energy we cultivate. By aligning with abundance in all areas of his life, George created a fertile ground for himself, and others to be abundant, and flourish. He became his own supporter and critic, celebrating and improving at the same time. Now the truth, the way you see life is the way you see yourself; life reflects the way you are and how you see it.

By embracing holistic wealth and collaborating with like-minded individuals, we create a powerful synergy that propels us toward lasting financial success. Recognize the value of nurturing your holistic well-being and forging empowering connections. By doing so, you create a solid foundation for prosperity and open yourself up to a world of limitless possibilities. True abundance is not a destination but a life-long journey, and the best is yet to come. George is going to make these teachings available.

This was the way to show everyone it works. I dare people to try. He said. I will prove them wrong as always.

"The last secret of the Son/Sun of God.

George began telling a story,

In the beginning, when the world was young and darkness blanketed the earth, a divine plan was set in motion". he said, telling a story from the archive. Describing the world means your reality, the earth is your mind". "The heavens whispered secrets to the hearts of the chosen, revealing a profound truth that would shape the course of humanity for eternity" George broke down the meaning again, saying the heavens are consciousness whispering, God is you in this story.

In the celestial realm, where stars shimmered like jewels, God beheld the plight of humankind, meaning ideas and thoughts. The world had lost its way, consumed by darkness, fear, and despair. God's heart ached for His children, yearning to bring them back into the embrace of His love and light. George again describes that thoughts were God's children left in darkness, fear, and despair.

The author continues to tell the story.

In this moment of divine compassion, God decided to send forth His only begotten Son as a beacon of hope and salvation. This Son would be the embodiment of divine love and wisdom, a radiant light within the hearts of humanity.

A spark of the divine, woven from the very essence of God's love. He would descend from the heavens to walk amongst mortals, carrying the torch of divine consciousness, and guiding them back to the path of truth and enlightenment.

In the fullness of time, the son was born into the world, heralded by a celestial symphony of angels. His birth was not grand, for His purpose was not to claim dominion over empires but to reign down the hearts of humanity. George explained that the Son represents the penial gland, and described how it shines electromagnetically. The electricity rains up and down the charkas.

As the Son grew, His divine light radiated from every pore of His being. He performed miracles that defied the limitations of the physical realm, healing the sick, giving sight to the blind, and raising the fallen.

Yet, His mission extended far beyond miraculous acts. It was to inspire a transformation within each soul, to remind them of their true nature - divine, limitless, and connected to the Creator.

His words were like seeds sown upon fertile soil, sprouting into mighty trees of wisdom that would bear fruit for generations to come.

Yet, the journey of the Son was not without challenges. He faced resistance from those who clung to the darkness of ignorance and fear. His message threatened the established order, shaking the foundations of their limited beliefs.

As the Son approached the culmination of His earthly mission, He faced a defining moment. In the garden of Gethsemane, He prayed for strength and guidance, knowing that the path before Him was one of great sacrifice.

In a profound act of love, the Son willingly laid down His life for the redemption of humanity. He surrendered to the fate that awaited Him, knowing that his physical form would pass, but His eternal light would continue to shine as a guiding star for all.

Upon the cross, the Son radiated a brilliance that pierced the veil of darkness, illuminating the hearts of all who beheld His sacrifice. In that sacred moment, humanity witnessed the triumph of love over hate, of light over darkness.

And so, the Son's physical form returned to the heavens, but His light remained, imprinted upon the collective consciousness of humanity.

As the story unfolds, George explains that the Son was not sent to be worshipped as a distant deity, but to be recognized as the light within every soul and mind. He came not to be an intermediary between humanity and God, but to be the embodiment of the eternal truth that dwells within each of us.

George explained the Son is a story of hope, love, and the eternal journey of the soul toward its divine source. It is a story of the light within, guiding us back to the mind of God, where we find ourselves, ultimate peace, in joy, and fulfillment. This is where you heard the phrase "Know Thy Self" because knowing yourself is knowing God.

With each passing scroll, George learns that the First Dynasty Mindset is not merely a philosophy but a transformative way of being - a journey that leads to the awakening of the pineal gland. As he absorbs the sacred teachings, he comes to understand the profound connection between his thoughts and the reality he experiences.

In the secluded solitude of his chamber, George delves deeper into the rituals and practices passed down from his ancestors. He begins to activate the pineal gland through focused intention, meditation, and sacred techniques. As he opens this portal of divine consciousness, a flood of spiritual energy surges through him, connecting him to the higher truths of existence.

As days turn into nights, George witnesses the world around him with new eyes. He feels a profound oneness with the universe, understanding that the "only begotten Son" is not just a historical tale but a representation of the divine essence within each soul.

George believed with this understanding he had the power of God inside his mind. We somehow cut off ourselves from believing in ourselves, but it is true, the power was in our minds, and I intend to use that power. We are to follow God in Heaven our Father like dear children the bible says. How do we imitate the Father our God in heaven?

God calls the unseen to be seen. George's answer was to have faith in our beliefs, our potential, and our ability to be abundant because that is calling the unseen to be seen, like God. For faith is the substance of things hoped for, and the evidence of things unseen. He finished his story and left his mother in shock and awe.

At large, he remains committed to empowering individuals to unlock their inner light, transform their lives, and embrace the boundless possibilities that lie within them. Through his profound words and inspiring presence, George is dedicated to leaving a legacy of positive change and spiritual growth for generations to come.

11

FIRST DYNASTY: THE LIGHT WITHIN - IGNITING THE ETERNAL FLAME OF ABUNDANCE

FIRST DYNASTY: The Light Within - Igniting the Eternal Flame of Abundance

George's awe-inspiring journey, we are reminded of the profound impact that the power of thought, the integration of the paradigm of thought, and the principles of the First Dynasty mindset continue to have on his life. Through his transformation, George not only unlocked his own wealth and abundance but also unlocked abundance and wealth for others, a beacon of inspiration for generations to come.

His story, infused with the essence of resilience and unwavering belief, has become a timeless source of motivation and empowerment. It is a testament to the indomitable human spirit and the boundless potential that lies within each one of us.

The time is now. He claims, embrace the light within and unleash your limitless potential. May your journey be filled with abundance, fulfillment, and the realization of your wildest dreams. The power is within you. You are the torchbearer of your destiny, and the world eagerly awaits the brilliance of your light.

Thank you for embarking on this extraordinary journey with us.

May your path be illuminated by the wisdom of the First Dynasty mindset, and may you forever bask in the radiant glow of abundance and prosperity.

12

POSTLOGUE

Beyond his writing, George actively engages with his community through workshops, seminars, and motivational speaking engagements. He is a beacon of hope for those seeking guidance on their personal development journey, providing them with practical tools and spiritual insights to navigate life's challenges with grace and resilience.

As George Dennis Jr. continues to make a significant impact on his community and the world at large, he remains committed to empowering individuals to unlock their inner light, transform their lives, and embrace the boundless possibilities that lie within them. Through his profound words and inspiring presence, he is dedicated to leaving a legacy of positive change and spiritual growth for generations to come.

13

FIRST DYNASTY MINDSET: A 7-DAY MEDITATION JOURNEY TO INNER TRANSFORMATION

Day 1: Awakening the Power within

Welcome to Day 1 of the First Dynasty Mindset Meditation Journey. Today marks the beginning of a profound transformation as we unlock the power within ourselves. Find a peaceful space where you can be free from distractions and close your eyes. Take deep, intentional breaths, inhaling positive energy, and exhaling any doubts or worries.

As you settle into a state of calm, focus your attention on your heart center—the source of your inner strength and intuition. Envision a radiant light glowing within your heart, symbolizing the limitless potential within you. Affirm: "I am a vessel of abundance and transformation. My thoughts shape my reality, and I attract positive opportunities."

Feel the energy of your heart expanding, radiating love and compassion. Embrace the potential for positive change in your life as you bask in the loving energy of your heart center.

Day 2: Embracing the Present Moment

On Day 2, we deepen our practice of the First Dynasty Mindset through mindfulness and presence. Begin the meditation by taking slow, deliberate breaths. Focus your attention on your breath, using it as an anchor to keep you rooted in the present moment.

As thoughts arise, observe them without judgment and gently bring your focus back to your breath. Embrace the serenity of the present, releasing attachments to the past and worries about the future. Find peace and clarity as you remain fully present.

Throughout the day, practice mindful awareness in your daily activities. Engage with the world around you without getting caught up in its distractions. Cultivate inner peace and clarity as you navigate your day.

Day 3: Cultivating Gratitude and Abundance

Gratitude is a potent tool to amplify the First Dynasty Mindset. Today, we focus on cultivating gratitude and appreciation. Begin by acknowledging three things you are grateful for in your life. Embrace the joy and abundance that gratitude brings.

As you express gratitude, feel your heart expanding with appreciation. Gratitude opens doors to abundance, attracting more of what you are thankful for. Embrace the feeling of gratitude and let it permeate your being.

Throughout the day, maintain an attitude of gratitude. Notice how this shift in perspective transforms your experiences, bringing more joy and fulfillment into your life.

Day 4: Visualization for Empowerment

Day 4 centers around the power of visualization to manifest your desires. Close your eyes and visualize your ideal self—the best version of you. See yourself achieving your goals with confidence and determination.

As you visualize, feel the emotions of accomplishment and fulfillment. Embrace the belief that your ideal self is within reach and that you are worthy of all your desires.

Throughout the day, revisit this visualization whenever doubt or negativity arises. By consistently focusing on your ideal self, you align your thoughts and actions with your dreams.

Day 5: Releasing Limiting Beliefs

Today, confront and release limiting beliefs that hinder your growth. During the meditation, bring to mind any negative beliefs that have influenced your actions in the past.

Visualize these beliefs as clouds dissipating into the sky, leaving your mind clear and free. Replace limiting beliefs with positive affirmations that empower and uplift you.

Throughout the day, challenge any negative thoughts or beliefs. Remind yourself of your newfound power to overcome them and embrace a more empowering mindset.

Day 6: Embracing Inner Wisdom

On Day 6, we connect with our inner wisdom, the guiding light within us. During the meditation, focus on your heart center once again. Envision a brilliant light shining from within, representing your inner wisdom.

Ask your inner wisdom for guidance on any challenges or decisions you face. Trust that the answers will come when the time is right and have faith in your intuition.

Throughout the day, practice tuning into your inner guidance. Let your intuition lead you toward a more aligned and purposeful life.

Day 7: Embodying Transformation

As we reach the final day of the First Dynasty Mindset Meditation Journey, we embrace the transformation that has taken place within us. Reflect on the insights and growth you have experienced throughout the past week.

Close your eyes and visualize yourself stepping into a new chapter of life—a chapter filled with confidence, purpose, and abundance. Embrace the changes that have occurred and affirm your commitment to continued growth.

As you conclude this meditation, express gratitude for the journey you have embarked on. Carry the lessons and wisdom with you as you move forward, knowing that the power to transform your life lies within you.

IN CONCLUSION:

Congratulations on completing the First Dynasty Mindset Meditation Journey. Remember that this is just the beginning of your transformative path. Continue to practice these meditation techniques and embrace the First Dynasty Mindset as you navigate your life's journey.

Let the light within guide you toward a future filled with abundance, joy, and fulfillment. Embrace your true potential and watch as your life unfolds in magical ways.

May you walk the path of inner transformation with courage, grace, and an unwavering belief in your infinite possibilities. Your destiny awaits—embrace the Light within and let it shine brightly for all the world to see.

14

MASTERING YOUR INNER DIALOGUE: A 14-DAY CHALLENGE FOR INNER TRANSFORMATION

Welcome to the "Mastering Your Inner Dialogue" 14-Day Challenge—a transformative journey towards harnessing the power of your thoughts and unlocking your true potential. Your inner dialogue, the constant stream of thoughts and self-talk that runs through your mind, plays a significant role in shaping your beliefs, actions, and ultimately, your reality. By mastering your inner dialogue, you gain the key to creating positive changes and manifesting abundance in all aspects of your life.

Day 1: Awakening Awareness

Begin your journey by bringing awareness to your inner dialogue. Take a few moments of quiet reflection and observe the thoughts that arise in your mind. Are they empowering or limiting? Notice any patterns or recurring themes. Today, you lay the foundation for transforming your self-talk into a powerful ally.

Day 2: Identifying Limiting Beliefs

On Day 2, delve deeper into your inner dialogue to identify any limiting beliefs that may be holding you back. These beliefs often arise from past experiences or external influences and can create barriers to your growth. Recognize them for what they are—false narratives that no longer serve you.

Day 3: Reframing Limiting Beliefs

Having identified limiting beliefs, it's time to reframe them into empowering statements. Challenge each negative belief and transform it into a positive affirmation. For example, replace "I am not good enough" with "I am worthy of success and happiness." Embrace the power of positive self-talk and internalize these empowering affirmations.

Day 4: Cultivating Self-Compassion

Self-compassion is vital in mastering your inner dialogue. Today, practice being kind and understanding towards yourself. When negative thoughts arise, respond with self-compassion and gentleness. Treat yourself as you would a close friend, offering encouragement and support.

Day 5: Embracing Gratitude

Gratitude has the power to shift your inner dialogue towards positivity. Take time to reflect on all the blessings in your life and express gratitude for them. As you cultivate a grateful mindset, watch how your inner dialogue transforms, attracting even more abundance and positivity.

Day 6: Visualization for Empowerment

Visualization is a powerful tool for mastering your inner dialogue. Close your eyes and visualize yourself confidently achieving your goals and dreams. Engage all your senses and feel the emotions of success. This practice rewires your mind for success and aligns your inner dialogue with your desired outcomes.

Day 7: Nurturing Self-Love

Today, nurture self-love and acceptance. Embrace your unique qualities and recognize your strengths. Celebrate your successes and forgive yourself for past mistakes. Love yourself unconditionally and let that love radiate through your inner dialogue.

Day 8: Cultivating Mindfulness

Mindfulness anchors you in the present moment, reducing the chatter of your inner dialogue. Practice mindfulness throughout the day by focusing on your breath, sensations, or surroundings. Observe your thoughts without judgment, allowing them to come and go like passing clouds.

Day 9: Embracing Positive Affirmations

Affirmations are powerful tools to reinforce positive beliefs. Create a list of empowering affirmations aligned with your goals and values. Repeat them throughout the day, replacing any negative self-talk with these uplifting statements.

Day 10: Journaling for Clarity

Journaling helps gain clarity on your thoughts and emotions. Take time to write down your inner dialogue, exploring the root of any negative patterns. Use this practice as a therapeutic way to release pent-up emotions and gain insights into your thought processes.

Day 11: Empowering Your Inner Champion

Today, channel your inner champion—your inner voice of encouragement and inspiration. Whenever self-doubt arises, call upon your inner champion to affirm your capabilities and strengths. Trust that you have the power to overcome challenges and achieve your goals.

Day 12: Embracing Positivity

Surround yourself with positive influences. Engage with uplifting books, podcasts, or inspirational content that reinforces a positive mindset. By immersing yourself in positivity, you strengthen your inner dialogue with empowering beliefs.

Day 13: Revisiting Your Progress

Take time to reflect on your journey so far. Notice the changes in your inner dialogue and how they have impacted your thoughts, feelings, and actions. Celebrate your growth and acknowledge any areas that may still require nurturing.

Day 14: Integration and Gratitude

As you near the end of the challenge, integrate the lessons learned into your daily life. Continue practicing self-awareness, positive affirmations, and mindfulness. Express gratitude for the transformation that has taken place within you and maintain your commitment to mastering your inner dialogue.

~

Congratulations on completing the "Mastering Your Inner Dialogue" 14-Day Challenge. By mastering your inner dialogue, you have unlocked the doorway to creating a life of abundance, joy, and fulfillment. Remember that this journey is ongoing, and each day presents an opportunity for growth and transformation.

As you move forward, hold onto the power of positive self-talk and affirmations. Embrace your inner champion, and let your thoughts become a magnet for opportunities and success. Trust that by nurturing your inner dialogue, you have the ability to manifest your deepest desires and create the life you envision.

May the First Dynasty Mindset continue to guide you on your path to inner transformation, empowering you to shine your light brightly and positively impact the world around you. Embrace the power within, for it is the key to living a life of purpose and joy.

15

DYNASTY MINDSET QUOTES TO OVERCOME SELF-LIMITING BELIEFS.

Day 1: "The power of my thoughts shapes my reality. I choose to focus on abundance and attract endless opportunities." – Dynasty Mindset.

Day 2: "As I master my inner dialogue, I become the grand architect of my life, creating a life of purpose, fulfillment, and abundance." – Dynasty Mindset

Day 3: " Thoughts are the seeds of my reality. With positivity and intention, I sow the garden of my reality." – Dynasty Mindset.

Day 4: "Every morning, I align my thoughts with my vision, drawing the energy I need towards my goals." - Dynasty Mindset.

Day 5: "With gratitude, I celebrate the abundance that surrounds me and invite even more abundance into my world." - Dynasty Mindset.

Day 6: "As the master of my mind, by delegating my thoughts towards greatness and success brings fulfillment in every journey." - Dynasty Mindset.

Day 7: "Through visualization, I paint the canvas of my future on the space of reality, filling it with vivid colors of achievement, prosperity, and wholeness" – Dynasty Mindset.

Day 8: "Mindfulness grounds me in the present, gratefulness, and

35

visions of the future freed me from past limitations and past anxieties." - Dynast Mindset.

Day 9: "My worthiness is affirmed, and I embrace my uniqueness, knowing that I am destined for better things life has to offer" – Dynasty Mindset.

Day 10: "In the book of my life, I find clarity, healing, and the wisdom to navigate my journey with grace." - Dynasty Mindset.

Day 11: "I call on the higher version of myself to rise above challenges, empowering me to triumph against all odds." – Dynasty Mindset.

Day 12: "I surround myself with positivity and inspiration, I fuel my inner dialogue with the belief that anything is possible." - Dynasty Mindset.

Day 13: "I reflect on my progress, acknowledge my growth, and commit to self-improvement." -Dynasty Mindset.

Day 14: "Thankfulness and gratitude become my daily meditation, replenishing my soul and elevating my mind." - Dynasty Mindset.

Day 15: "My thoughts create reality, shaping my life and the life of others, making the world a fulfilling and abundant existence." – Dynasty Mindset.

Day 16: "With undying faith, I manifest my desires and wishes, knowing that the universe conspires to bring them to reality." -– Dynasty Mindset.

Day 17: "Through my thoughts, I transcend limitations and open the door to unlimited opportunities." - Dynasty Mindset.

Day 18: "I release all doubts, anxiety, and fears, allowing the power of my thoughts to guide me towards prosperity." - Dynasty Mindset.

Day 19: "Each morning, with intention, I align my thoughts for the life I envision myself." - Dynasty Mindset.

Day 20: "I choose self-compassion, embracing my imperfections and celebrating my achievements during my journey." - Dynasty Mindset.

Day 21: "My thoughts are the sacred gift, and I use them to co-create a reality that serves my highest vision and the greater advancement of the mind and spirit." - Dynasty Mindset.

Day 22: "I am the conscious creator, and with every thought, I shape the masterpiece of my reality." - – Dynasty Mindset.

Day 23: "Grateful for the lessons of the past, I let go of the Old Testament and welcome the New Testament of the present." - Dynasty Mindset.

Day 24: "Change allows me to harness the energy of transformation and unlock new opportunities for transcendence." - – Dynasty Mindset.

Day 25: "With I think with an open heart and mind, I command abundance to flow into every part of my life." - – Dynasty Mindset.

Day 26: "I see challenges as stepping stones, propelling me towards greatness and purpose." - – Dynasty Mindset.

Day 27: "My thoughts are a magnet, attracting the experiences and people that align with my highest vision." - Dynasty Mindset.

Day 28: "Through the art of visualization, I create a vision on the space of reality, my dreams are displayed on the screen of possibilities, igniting the flame of creative passion within my mind, so reality comes true" - – Dynasty Mindset.

Day 29: "Mindfulness and awareness of my thoughts, allows me to release the past and savor the present, making way for an abundant future." - – Dynasty Mindset.

Day 30: "I am the source of inspiration, spreading positivity and uplifting others through the power of my thoughts." - Dynasty Mindset.

9 789655 784190